CHOSEN FROM BIRTH

CHOSEN
FROM
BIRTH

Vera Simpson Gaines
& Bonnie Davis

authorHOUSE®

AuthorHouse™ LLC
1663 Liberty Drive
Bloomington, IN 47403
www.authorhouse.com
Phone: 1-800-839-8640

Published by AuthorHouse 03/13/2014

ISBN: 978-1-4918-5752-6 (sc)
ISBN: 978-1-4918-5751-9 (e)

FOREWORD

This has to be one of the most heartbreaking, compelling stories I've ever read. I did not have the privilege of knowing Bonnie Davis. Bonnie's husband Jim was the head carpenter on our lodge and one day out of the blue Jim asked me to review Bonnie's notes and see if I thought it was good enough to turn into a book. On Bonnie's death bed, she asked Jim to make sure her story be told which was her dream. Bonnie wanted to reach out to help others who have suffered like her. Bonnie wants people to know that if she can survive her horrible ordeal that anyone can survive with the help of God. Bonnie spent a lot of time reading her bible along with self-help books and therapy. I can truthfully say she conquered her past. Unfortunately, Bonnie died in July, 2009 of cancer. Here lies Bonnie's last dying wish. Her story.

Vera Simpson Gaines

Take my yoke upon
you and learn from
me, for I am gentle
and lowly in heart,
and you will find
rest for your souls.
Matthew 11:29

Chapter 1

My name is Bonnie Davis and I was born in 1963 a poor farmer's daughter. By poor, I mean there was no extra money. There was plenty of food since we grew our own vegetables and processed our own meat, as did most people back in the day. We lived in rural north Mississippi and most of our relatives lived on the same road, only yards apart.

I didn't mind the gardening, although I must admit that working truck patches was not as much fun as a smaller garden. I did, however, very much enjoy the processing of our own meats. Hogs were always killed and processed in the fall of the year. I loved the smell of lard cooking over that big open fire in the cool crisp fall air. My dad raised pigs and ran a dairy as well as farmed about 1,000 acres of land. Dad came from a long line of farmers. He was stocky built and had big strong arms and hands. He was a very good looking man. He was a respectable man even though he was a week-end alcoholic. He was generous and quiet natured. He was a hard worker and taught me how to work hard. He gave me life in more than one way. He protected me as best he could from the harsh coldness of my mother. I could always count on Daddy for anything I needed. He was trustworthy and most of the time easy to talk to. He was the best Dad God could have given a little girl like me and I loved him with all my heart.

Mom was resentful with her life style and was powerless to change it. She was a small built woman and very nice looking. There were two different sides to her. In public, she was nice but behind closed doors she was a monster. She was deeply disturbed. Manic depressive in my mind.

I knew Mother as a lair by the time I was 5 yrs. old and understood her manipulations by the age of 8. She was a good mother to my siblings. She didn't like her own mother and shut her out of her life, but she loved her Daddy very much. I always wondered what issues she had with her own mother. Grandma never liked to talk about Mom so I can only speculate what problems they had between them.

1963 was the year John F. Kennedy was shot. It was a busy and ever changing world. With the nation on its way to super power status, I can remember the women's liberation movement and man landing on the moon in 1969. Factories were the only primary source of income around our parts. Cars were big. Gas was only 95 cents a gallon and people still complained. Clothing stores were a privilege. Sears was the first store we ordered our supplies from. If you didn't like Sears, then you were out of luck or you learned to make your own clothes. The catalog was the wish book.

I remember when my daddy bought the first cotton picker. All came out to see it and watched him operate it. No one had ever seen something so high tech before. It was amazing and gone were the endless days of picking cotton by hand. I can remember acres and acres of cotton fields littered with people dragging their cotton sacks in the heat of the day with no breeze in sight. It was stifling work and no one was exempt. I think that the awesome machine brought freedom to lots of people while it probably starved others. I think it was a bitter sweet deal in the name of progress.

There was a world of difference in the way the children responded to their parents. If I had talked back to my parents I would not be alive today. Children need to learn to respect their elders. If a child is not taught by the age of ten to respect authority then they will end up in trouble with the law.

Back in the day, if you got in trouble at school then you got in trouble with your parents when you got home. Children also need to be raised in church. My parents didn't raise me in church and I would have loved it. I had to learn the bible as an adult so I missed all the bible stories and all the fun activities that the other children were doing.

Jesus said, "With men
it is impossible, but
not with God, because
all things are possible
with God."
Mark 10:27

Chapter 2

In researching some of my daddy's roots, I discovered that there are two sides to his family. One was a bootlegger side while the other side was a preacher's side. My daddy's side was the bootlegger side which explains a lot of why my daddy was an alcoholic. He was not a hell raising drunk. He would give you his last quarter if you asked him for it. He was loved by all who knew him except for my mother. Dad was a very hard worker and he expected everyone to pull their share. Dad would come in from the fields on Friday afternoon and would leave and not come back until Sunday night. He would go to his family's farm, where they made their whiskey. He would take the only vehicle we had. Mother hated him for leaving her home alone with 4 kids to tend to. I imagine she got real lonely without another adult to talk to. I felt sorry for her. She would get even with him eventually. Not a good way to have a marriage.

No one gets to pick the family they are born into. You have to learn how to adjust to your surroundings. Unfortunately, I had to learn this at a very young age to survive. You will learn in the course of this book the damage it does to one's soul not to have the love of both parents. Let me make it clear that even though my mother hated me, I still loved her very much and desperately wanted her love and attention, more than anyone will ever know.

Everyone assumes a baby will be loved and nurtured by their birth mother, but that is not true in my case. A baby should bring joy to the family. From day one my mother didn't want anything to do with me for the simple reason that I looked like my dad. Have you heard of anything so insane?

Dad's family didn't take things out on me for looking like him. I'm glad there are a lot of things I don't remember because of my young age. There was plenty to remember that I wish I had forgotten! Everything that happens to you is recorded and stored somewhere in the brain. Sometimes a sight, smell or touch can bring those memories to the front of the brain. Wouldn't it be nice if we could erase those bad memories?

I will
not
leave
you.
Genesis 28: 15

Chapter 3

I was marked from the beginning because I looked just like my dad. People would say I was a clone of my dad from day one. My earliest memory of abuse came when I was around 2 yrs. old. I remember an old lady in a squeaking wooden rocking chair. She is rocking me and singing a gospel song. She would lean forward and I would vomit into an old silver rusty bucket. I would vomit and she would lay me back in her arms and wipe my face with a rag. She kept rocking me and singing for what seemed like days. I learned much later at 16 yrs. of age who the woman was. She was a neighbor of ours.

I was told that my sister who was a year older was the one that handed me the glass of clorox to drink and it nearly killed me. I searched my memory for the truth. I thought I remembered leaning against the door facing to the utility room, but there was no facing to that room. What I was actually holding on to was my mother's legs. I think my mother handed me the glass instead of my sister. I figure she was going to blame it on Christy because who would punish a 3 yr. old for murder.

No one was ever told about the incident because I stayed at the neighbor's house till right before my father came home on Sunday night. My grandmother would have carried me to the hospital if she had known. I think my mother expected me to die and she would have blamed my sister for my death. I was so upset to learn that my mother hated me that much. Mother ripped my guts out. I had no recollection of my mother ever touching me in a loving way.

She doted on my siblings and would make sure I saw her.

Those flashbacks rung my heart out like a wet sponge. How could this be? Why would a mother hate her own child's face? It was so hard to accept, but as absurd as it sounds, that's exactly the way it was. I had asked God my whole life, why?

"Why me, God?" I would beg over and over. The answers were already inside of me. Through meditation and in reverence God revealed the truth to me. That rattled me to the core of my being. Why, doesn't matter. Why will never matter. Why it happened isn't the real issue. What did matter was how I viewed it. What mattered even more were all the wrongs I had committed against God because of the abuse. Nothing's more humbling than having your transgressions spilled out before you, like a big dam bursting. For the first time, I understood that my sins were not the heinous act. My sins were all the wrong choices I had made stemmed from the abuse. Having my dam burst like that was violent at the start and like any breach in a dam, once it burst, all the water gushed forward relieving some of the pressure.

Even though I was sorrowed by what had happened to me, I still didn't like it. I faced it head on. Afterwards, I felt more alive than ever before.

The pain gave way to acceptance and that opened the flood gates that allowed me a taste of forgiveness for the vey first time from God's well of mercy and grace. Just enough to moisten the parched edges of my cracked and split soul. The first sip, but not the last. Some people may wonder why I needed forgiveness. After all I was just a baby and it wasn't my fault. In one sense, they are right. I think to myself, "Look at you." Although, I was a baby when my mother tried to kill me, now I'm that baby all grown up and the anger still burned.

My awful sins were selfish rage and anger. Abused from the age of 2 yrs. old to present day. I had every reason to be angry and I had plenty of it. God opened my eyes to His truth concerning my attitude. I possess a spirit and a soul. The spirit hears with a different ear and the soul is healed upon God's command only! The human ear hears and supplies the information to your humanity. The spirit hears and then applies the truth to your soul for the sake of your salvation. It was my very salvation that was in the gravest danger.

Admitting my mother's role in the damage to my soul was a major step forward in my healing. Accepting that she had set me up for awful events that plagued the first eight years of my life was a big chunk to swallow. The memories of those days haunted me for the next 35 yrs. of my life.

It was an elaborate scheme manipulated by the devil, himself.

Created from evil and fed by Mother's hatred. She literally had two faces. She put on one very convincing show in public, pretending to be this sweet, respectable, caring wife and mother, but behind closed doors, she was quite the opposite. At times, you could taste the sugar that oozed from her pores and at other times, she was like a raging cat. Out of control, ranting, and raving, like two cats about to fight. Right before they pounce, they do this ritualistic sort of dance that seems to warn the other cat, "I'm mad! I'm fixing to hurt you! You better back off!" With their faces all snarling and distorted, ears laid back, hair standing on end while making some kind of eerie, elongated, uncomfortable meow like whining sound.

My Mom's darker side was every bit as viscous as her sweet side was fake. Struggling to forgive my mother for her part in those horrors would take me to the brink of literal death. This is a true account of what God did with a life that was marked for evil before birth and His triumphant victory over evil in the end. Don't people know that Christ defeated Satan on the cross. Satan is defeated and he knows it.

Salvation is free. You don't have to earn it. There is nothing here on earth that you could do to deserve it. Jesus gave his life so that you could live with Him in heaven. All you have to do is ask Him into your heart. Confess your sins and turn from evil. If you've lost a child, don't you want to live forever with that child in heaven? Don't leave this earth without Jesus!

Faith is the substance
of things hoped for,
the evidence of
things not seen.
Hebrews 11: 1

Chapter 4

My mother did as she chose to me. Back in the day, nobody questioned the so-call discipline. I call it child abuse. There were always fights over me. My daddy objected to the harsh beatings. He laid down the law to her, but it actually made it worse. I was too little to understand why my name was mentioned during all the fights, hollering, cussing, and throwing things. When I asked my sister what was going on, she always said she didn't know. After so many arguments, do you think she really didn't know? I knew she was lying. I tried to force it out of her but she never told me what was going on. I thought we had a normal family because that was all I knew. Now that I know, I'm proud of Daddy for standing up for me.

All this made Mom more determined and sneaky and she found really low ways to hurt me. I had no way to prove what she was doing to me. I couldn't fight back or disrespect her or rebel against her. I just had to take it. I got smarter as I grew and I made it harder for her to catch me in any kind of trap. I spent a lot of time figuring out ways to protect myself from her. Her abuse never did fully stop until her death.

They say that the eyes are the windows to the soul. My Mom had dark, cold eyes. If I dared to look her in the eyes, she would jump up and beat me so bad. It was like she knew I saw evil in her eyes. I learned very quickly not to look her in the eyes. She had the most evil eyes I have ever seen.

I saw her crying to herself on occasion. The only time I can remember her being happy was in my early teens. She was caught by Daddy having an affair with a man she worked with at the factory.

When I look back at my family, they were all so uneducated and ignorant in lots of ways. My brother quit school before he reached high school. My sister Christy graduated with pictures, invitations and the whole nine yards. I was sent my diploma in the mail the same year Christy graduated with a letter stating that I had too many credits. You only needed 16 credits to graduate and in my junior year I had 24 credits. Say goodbye to school and the only hope or outlet I had with civilization.

I don't want to be like the rest of the world. I want something more. I don't want to deny the truth or to run from it. I will not hide from shame or humility. I will not live as a dead woman walking. I will face my adversaries head on. I want to feel all that I can and am able. I want to cry with the ones who grieve in utter sorrow. I want to laugh and dance with the ones who whole heartily and soulfully rejoice for the good of another. I want to live the life God has allotted me. I want to reach out beyond my dark boundaries and live the life I was meant to live. I want to be a breath of fresh air to the depressed and down trodden. I want to be a light for those who live in the dark unbeknownst to themselves. All of this I can and will be for God has so graced me. May I never be accused of not caring for the betterment or uplifting of others. I have lived to help those who can not help themselves. For the ones in the valley of the shadow of their own deaths, I pray that God allows me to be the cushion on which they lay their heads and a blanket to warm them. I ask not to spare them from their journey, only that I might be allowed to comfort them along the way. I want to comfort those who have been abused. I want to help people set the damaged child trapped inside free. Healing has to begin from the inside out. Keeping the abuse secret is the worse thing one can do to themselves. I was forced to keep my mouth shut. Find someone to talk to.

But continue thou
in the things which
thou hast learned and
hast been assured of
knowing of whom
thou hast learned them.
2 Timothy 3: 14

Chapter 5

I hated these three words, "You are so pretty." Sometimes that meant something else but I was too young to tell the difference. In time I learned the differences. I was around 4 yrs. old and the family was so excited because family from AR was coming. I didn't know them, but I would never soon forget them.

The oldest boy must have been a teenager because he was strong enough to pick me up and carry me where ever he wanted to take me. He would just stare at me and I didn't understand his gaze, but his attention or infatuation with me bothered me greatly. The next day this relative picked me up and carried me to the woods. He told the other children to play hide and go seek while he babysat me. As soon as they started counting, he took off with me and hid behind a big tree. That is when he first raped me. The next day they came and I ran and hid under my bed. My mother came in my room and dragged me outside. She pushed me out the door and locked it. The whole time I'm begging her not to make me go outside. She told me to go play with my relatives. She would beat me if I didn't go.

He came running around the corner of the house, and grabbed me. He said, "We're going to have fun!" He picked me up and carried me to the barn laying me down on a bail of hay. He raped me again. I was crying and begging him to please stop. Finally he stopped. He was furious! He took me by the arm and dragged me back to the house. He told my mother that I was scared and wouldn't stop crying. Mom grabbed me by the hair and slammed the door. She dragged me into my bedroom and stripped off my clothes. She beat me so bad! She beat me long and hard. She told me I was being hateful and stubborn toward our relatives. She told me to get dressed.

I stayed in my room the rest of the day. I avoided Mother at all cost. I didn't say a word. I was confused about what had happened to me over the last two days. I didn't understand why he kept doing those things to me. The whole time he is saying how pretty I am. I hated pretty! I prayed for God to make me ugly so he would stop.

I remember when they left. I stood there in some kind of trance. They loaded up their truck and headed home to AR. I always wondered if Mom knew what was going on. How could she not know?

One time I remember there was a cool fall evening and we were sitting on the steps by the kitchen door. They were all huddled up together and I was cold. One of my siblings got up and I moved into their place. Mom pushed me away from her. I fell into the space between the steps and the brick. I got stuck and they just laughed at me. It skinned my back and hip so bad, but did they care. No! They wouldn't even help me out of the hole. When I finally got out, I ran to the bathroom to look at my injuries. How can people be so cruel? It was so clear how much they hated me. I started wetting the bed after the rapes. Mom would beat me but I didn't know how to make it stop. I prayed for God to help me make it stop. Was He really there? Was He listening to my prayers?

Mom went to work at the furniture frame factory and a black woman came to keep us. Everyday she would strip the sheets and I would get a whipping for wetting the bed. If I didn't start crying immediately she would keep on beating me till I did. One day I decided that I was going to be a big girl and not cry. I was beaten so bad but I did not cry one tear. She kept beating me till she got tired and stopped.

The next day she was going to beat me again for wetting the bed yet again but when she pulled down my pants she saw how bruised I was and decided not to whip me. While we were outside playing the dog dug up a skunk. It sprayed our dog and talk about the smell!! She stripped off our clothes and put them in the wash. She made us stand on the front porch buck naked. At that moment, Daddy drove by the house and saw us naked on the front porch and boy did he blow a fuse. We never saw her again.

Another black lady came to keep us and she was so sweet. She would wash my sheets and tell me it wasn't my fault. Everything around our house was my fault according to my mother and siblings. I didn't understand why she didn't beat me like everybody else. I loved her!

My siblings were always getting me in trouble. They would tell Mom it was my fault and she believed them every time. Another reason to beat me and it would be double if David was involved. I remember one time David tore the arms and legs off my Barbie and we had a big fight. I punched David in the face and we rolled on the floor till

I could break free. I ran into the kitchen where Mom was cooking. I stopped right in front of her and turned just as David hit me in the stomach. He knocked the breath out of me and I fell to the floor. Mom and David just stood there laughing at me. I thought I was going to die. I needed her to help me. Why wouldn't she help me?

I got up and ran to my room slamming the door behind me. Mom was hot on my heels. She beat me so bad. She never asked me what David had done. Of course she didn't care, he was her favorite. He would have lied if she had asked. What's the use? Dad found out about the fight and he told Mom if she whipped me then she had to whip David as well or he would do it when he got home. Mom said David was her baby. Come on. Who are you trying to kid? He is the oldest. It made me sick every time I heard her say that. I'm proud of dad for standing up to her. It didn't do any good. Actually, it made things worse for me. If only Dad had known what all I endured when he wasn't there. Unfortunately, Daddy didn't know even half of it. I couldn't tell him because it would have made things worse for me. If I could have snapped my fingers, I would have changed everyone except my Dad. I loved my dad more than anything I knew. Sometimes I thought it would have been better to never have been born. That wasn't my choice was it?

You are with me;
your rod and staff,
they comfort me.
Psalm 23: 4

Chapter 6

I was spending the night with Grandmother when suddenly my Dad's brother came busting in the house screaming cuss words. It was about ten o'clock at night because the news was on in the living room where I had made a pallet to sleep on. I don't know what they were screaming about. All of a sudden he came in the room and grabbed me and threw me over his shoulder and headed for the door with my grandmother on his heels. She was begging him to put me down. He kept walking to his truck. I remember grandmother holding on to the screen door as we pulled out of the driveway. He had been drinking. I could smell it. He took me to his house. He immediately stripped me of my clothes. He forced my head down. I gagged so bad that I almost threw up. I was only 4 yrs. old so I had no idea what he was doing or what he expected me to do. Next he made me sit on his lap. I couldn't get away from him but when he went into the kitchen to get another beer, I bolted out the door. I ran as fast and hard as I could. I heard him come out the door because it slammed behind him. He cranked his truck and headed in my direction. I dove for the ditch and that's when I realized I didn't have on any clothes. My feet were bleeding from the rocks and my bottom was bleeding. I lay as still as I could even holding my breath when the truck came near and went real slow looking for me. After he passed, I ran into the woods running full speed in the dark and couldn't see a thing until I ran head on into a tree. It almost knocked me out. I laid there for a while till I could resume running the back way to my house.

When I reached the back door it was locked. I checked the other doors and they were locked as well. My only option was to sleep in the car. There was an old t-shirt of Dad's on the back seat so I pulled it over my head. I was freezing to death!

I huddled on the floor of the car curled up in a ball trying to keep warm. I don't think I got much sleep. I was just waiting for dawn to come so I could get in the house.

Mom made a comment about me being up early. I got a rag and cleaned up and headed to my room to find some clean clothes. I heard a truck pull up and men screaming at each other. I looked out the window and saw Daddy picking several switches off the tree. I knew somebody was in serious trouble. Dad grabbed me by my hair and dragged me to the back room. He was screaming some words but I didn't know what they meant. Words like whore, slut, and nasty. I knew nasty meant something like flies sitting on something. I would have to find out what those words meant so I wouldn't ever do that again.

My daddy used every switch on me until each one broke, then he pulled off his belt. The pain was more than I could bear and then something weird happened. The pain stopped and I noticed I was no longer in my body but crouched in the corner like an animal. I was watching my daddy beating me but there was no pain! Daddy kept on beating me till he was out of breath. Suddenly I returned to my body and the pain returned. My mom had stood there encouraging my dad on as he beat me. The pain was so extreme!

Mom asked Dad how he would like his eggs as if nothing had happened. I stayed in the room while the rest ate their breakfast. My younger brother slipped me some crumbs and I made sure none fell on the floor for Mom to see. It was only crumbs but it helped my stomach. I was so hungry!

I was trying to calm my breathing but it was extremely difficult. It had been a long horrible night and I will not forget it as long as I live! To this day, I can't stand to be cold, wet, or hungry because it brings back all those bad memories.

I looked into mom's vanity mirror and I didn't even recognize myself. I remember saying to myself, "Now you got blood all over the inside and outside!" I thought I was bleeding to death with blood running down the inside of my legs. I had marks all over my body that were bleeding. With all this blood on me I know I can't sit down or Mom would beat me. I can't take another beating. I get down on my knees and lean on my stomach. I'm so tired! I just want to go to sleep. I try to think what I have done wrong. I ran the words through my mind again trying to figure out what they meant. Since Daddy said nasty maybe it was because I didn't take a bath at grandmother's. That must be it. I was dirty!

Mom opened the door and I wanted to run to her. Instead she said in a very harsh voice to get in the bathroom and get cleaned up and then go to my room. As I walked through the door, she grabbed my shirt and shoved me into the bathroom and slammed the door. I once again got a rag and washed myself. I hurt all over to the point I didn't want to touch my body. I had whelps all over my body. I went into my bedroom and changed clothes and layed in the floor. We weren't allowed to lay on the bed after it had been made. I lay in the floor and colored while I held Susie Q in my arms trying to keep her from harm.

I fell asleep and when I woke up it was well into the afternoon. Mom opened my bedroom door and told me to stay in my room. I heard voices outside so I looked out my window to see a neighbor who was asking where I was. He was concerned about me because I had not been by in days to see him. It was nice to know someone cared enough to come by and ask about me. Mom told me I couldn't go over there anymore, but when she wasn't around I would slip over there to visit. Mr. Atlve was a fine Christian man. His wife was nice too. They use to tell me about Jesus since my family didn't take us to church.

From that day on things were never the same. Everybody would just look at me like I was something dirty or weird. I always felt like they were looking at me naked. It was because I was evil, nasty, a bitch, and a whore. I just wanted to be treated like everybody else. It seemed like all the dirty people came out of the woods and they wanted to have fun with me.

I learned to go home when it got dark. I needed a tree house to live in. That would have been perfect for me. I loved the gentle breeze that flowed through the trees. The fragrance of honeysuckle in the air with green onions and freshly cut grass filled my senses. I could smell the rain coming. The shadows that the tree branches created made good forms for creatures and other imaginary friends that I loved so dearly. Such peace. They say silence is golden. It truly is golden!

When I turned eight years old and started my periods, suddenly people no longer raped me but used other objects. They didn't want to get me pregnant. Even at school people didn't want to be near me or play with me. They acted like I would give them some kind of disease. I learned to play by myself like I did when I went to the woods behind our house.

But watch thou in all
things, endure afflictions,
do the work of an
evangelist, make full
proof of thy ministry.
2 Timothy 4: 5

Chapter 7

Dad started taking me to the fields with him. At first I thought it was to punish me but later I figured out what he was doing. Dad taught me how to work hard and how to do it right the first time. I was told to pick up the stumps and sticks out of the bottom land he had cleared. Then one day he took all four of us to the field. We were each given a certain section to clear. Later he would come back at lunch to check on us and our work. My section was just like he had taught me. The others had not cleared theirs. He jumped on all four of us and made us stay there till it was done right. I know that by all rights I should have been allowed to sit under the shade tree with him but he was teaching us a lesson.

Sometimes I finished a section before he came back and then I was allowed to sit with him under the shade tree. I went home when Daddy went home. The bottom line was Daddy was separating me from the others and keeping me away from Mom. Dad didn't know that the others were complaining to Mom when they got home, making things worse for me. I got beat for getting to sit in the shade with dad. I couldn't win for losing. Mom never needed an excuse. Anything she thought that was not fair to her favorites, was reason enough for her.

Relief came in the weirdest way in the year of 1974, when my grandfather died. It should have been a time of mourning but instead it provided freedom for me and my grandmother. My grandfather was mean to my grandmother. My grandmother was afraid to stay by herself at night so my dad allowed me to sleep over. I would do my chores and then head to grandmother's. I couldn't wait to get my chores done.

After the night of the rape I became fearful that it would happen again. My grandmother was no protection. It seemed like a door opened and there were so many people who wanted to abuse me. I felt like I was marked. I prayed for God to make me ugly so people would leave me alone. Please God, help me! I prayed for God to mess up my face. Here we go again saying how pretty I was. I didn't want to be pretty! I want to be ugly so they will go away!

Here comes the family from AR again. I would always hide when I heard them coming. I didn't want them to come for a visit. I tried to stay at my grandmother's but Mother wouldn't hear of it. She would drag me out from under my bed kicking and screaming. Out the door again and she would lock the door as usual. Same old routine as before!

My relative was always there waiting to carry me off to the woods. He would use his body parts and sticks on me. I can't wait for him to just get through. I'm looking away and thinking what I'm going to do when he gets through. I can't say how much bark I pulled out of me. I would itch real bad and there would be more bark. This is insane. I pray God is going to punish all my abusers!

When things would get too extreme for me I would leave my body, over and over again. I couldn't make myself do it. It would do it on its own. Something else did that. But when I left my body I couldn't feel the pain inflicted on my body until I returned to my body. When is this hell going to end? Why can't they see that I am a child and just leave me alone? Is this hell ever going to end for me or am I doomed? Why God are you allowing this to happen to me? I need you God to stop this madness. My family is killing me!

Let heaven fill your
thoughts. Do not think
only about things down
here on earth.
Colossians 3: 2

Chapter 8

Mom worked until 3:30 pm in a furniture frame factory and I tried hard to have my chores done as soon as possible. Divine intervention! My grandfather's death set me free and that was the best thing to ever happen to me. All the hate from Mom was replaced with love from grandmother. All the harsh ugly words and names were replaced by the sweetest voice I had ever heard to this day. All the slaps and whippings were replaced by huge hugs and kisses. All my wrongs were discussed at the kitchen table. She was always on my side. She directed me in the right way to go. All the hurtful, hateful, cruel words were replaced with words of encouragement and unconditional Christ-like, gentle loving words.

I loved my grandmother with all my heart. She never whipped me or raised her voice at me. She taught me how to cook, sew, clean, and how to avoid certain situations. Grandmother made me my very own pint sized cotton sack to pick cotton with. She had the biggest smile on her face when she placed it on my shoulder. I didn't have the heart to tell her I didn't want a baby sack. Now I couldn't get out of picking with my own sack. She meant well. She was a God send to me! Not one person ever talked bad about my grandmother except for my Mom, of course. Grandmother never said a bad word about anyone, esp. my mother. She was a true Christian lady in every sense of the word. She lived a tortured life and still held strong to her faith. She was the best role model I had. I still have grandmother's powder box. I loved the way she smelled. Every now and then I get the box out of my closet and just sit and smell the powder. It brings back wonderful memories of my beloved grandmother. She'll be waiting for me at the gate to heaven. What a beautiful sight that will be.

We walk
by faith,
not by sight.
2 Corinthians 5: 7

Chapter 9

Growing into my teen years, I wore average clothes so as not to call attention to myself. I was known as a tough girl. I fought everyday at school. The teachers finally got tired of spanking me and they would hit the bottom of their shoes so others would think I was getting spanked. Looking back now, I think my teachers saw things in me that helped them to extend their compassion to me.

I grew up during the desegregation of the schools. I had been raised prejudice, without knowing what it really was. It was normal to me. The blacks were made to come to our school and certain grades were made to go over to the black school. Wouldn't you know I was in the grade that had to move to the black school. When the black boys would walk down the hall they would put their hands on our butts. To me that was a fighting offense. My dad told my brother David that if he didn't take care of this situation that he would whip him when he got home from school. My brother got suspended a lot. Finally, I decided to take matters into my own hands. And boy did I!

I was called into the office one day in my sophomore year and they told me I was failing because I had missed too many days from being suspended. I maintained an average of A's and B's even with the zeros I received from the suspensions. Most of my teachers thought I must be a whiz kid to be able to do that. I could even sleep in class and the teachers would ask me a question and I still could give them the correct answers. It blew their minds. Finally, I think they figured things out. So the teachers decided to introduce me to literature and I loved it! The librarian at the high school was a god-send. She introduced me to all the classic books. Books of time I called them.

Moby Dick, The Call Of The Wild, and Shakespeare were some of my favorites. I loved her for what she did for me. My horizons expanded by leaps and bounds. There's another whole new world in books. It was a wonderful escape for me and others as well. I could pick up a book and travel the world at no charge. How awesome is that? Suddenly, I was someone else. I still love to read. I wore out that library. I figured I had only four years to read all the books on the shelves and I didn't waste any time.

I always had trouble with time. Don't know why but it was always a little off for me. I had an urgency about me to learn and grab all I could while I was able. I had a feeling that I would not be here long on this earth. I lived from minute to minute, never allowing myself to think about a future. What kind of future can you dream of when you are poor? I knew I would never be able to go to college because we didn't have any money. Who would want someone who got into so much trouble all the time? I had the ability to learn but no way to get there.

Man judges by the
outward appearance
but God judges
the heart.
unknown

Chapter 10

I was a sucker for an underdog because I grew up feeling like one. If I caught anyone trying to harm or making fun of anyone on the bus, I had to spring into action. I would come unglued! Naturally, I used my fists. Regardless of my good intentions, it was the wrong way to go about it.

There was this boy once that rode my school bus. He was thin and tall, but he had a mouth on him. His mouth was probably the biggest thing on the boy. One day on the bus he called my little brother a dumb-ass. That was his first mistake. I told him not to call my brother that again and well you can guess what he did. Yep. He made a very bad mistake.

As you well know the windows on the bus will only go half way down. I proceeded to stuff him out the window. I never said a word. I just kept pushing him out. You see I pushed his head out first so it was pretty easy to get the rest of him out the window. I was holding him by his ankles when the bus driver looked and saw what was going on. She immediately stopped the bus by slamming on her brakes, causing us to lunge forward. He hit the ground right beside the tire. He jumped up and came around and sat on the steps of the bus, afraid I was going to attack him again. He sat the seat right behind the bus driver. That's where he sat for the remainder of the school year. He never called anyone a bad name again.

I guess that's what gave me control of the bus. If I raised my arms out like I was going to fly off, a dead silence would come over the entire bus.

The power I achieved in such a short time was so amazing to me. He never said another word. Everyone acted like they didn't see or hear a thing.

If there ever was a mortifying moment on the bus it was when I was 16 yrs. old. A new boy moved into the area and he lived in this little shack stuck back up in the woods. The yard was never mowed and it looked like they had nailed shingles to the sides of the shack. Anyway, you get the picture. It wouldn't have even made a good dog house. But none the same he lived there. Our bus stopped to pick him up that first day and the bus fell deathly silent. We were in shock that anyone could live in that shack in those conditions. He was tall, maybe 5'7" or more. He wore Buddy Holly glasses with white adhesive tape holding on the sides. He had dark hair and fair skin. Honestly, it looked like he had pizza on his face. The acne was so bad! His parents couldn't afford a real house so you knew they couldn't afford any medicine for him.

His clothes were pitiful. Hand me downs, no doubt. He had no shame really because he was slightly retarded. This was all that the bullies needed to make fun of the boy. He was a good foot taller than me, but by birth he was only one year younger than me. He was teased and he would cry. I was smart enough to know I couldn't fix the world, but I had just about enough guts to try.

Well one day I get on the bus early. The older boys were already in their seats and so was the boy. They had taken his cap and were throwing it around the bus making the boy cry like a 4 yr. old. The boys laughed at him even harder and louder. Their first mistake was letting me see this. They were mocking him and I lost it. He definitely qualified for less fortunate and retarded.

I got up from my seat and walked over to the boy that had the hat. He thought I was going to hit him with my fist but I decided to box his ears instead. I hit him fast and hard. I didn't like him anyway so I tried to burst his eardrums. It can be done very easily if done right.

There was the cap on the floor at his feet. I couldn't reach it because he was in the way. So I quickly stepped behind his seat and grabbed a hand full of hair and jerked his head as hard as I could backwards. He sure didn't seem like such a bad ass now. I looked into his eyes with that look and calmly told him to pick up the cap and hand it to me right now. "You have four seconds when I let go or you are going to get hurt real bad," I said. His friend grabbed the cap and threw it at me like I was a vicious dog they were trying to get away from. I in turn handed the cap to the young boy. There is no need to torture people who can't defend themselves. That's the coward's way of doing things. It speaks volumes about your character.

Throw off all the
transgressions you
have committed,
and make yourselves
a new heart and
a new spirit.
Ezekiel 18:31

Chapter 11

If it was physical, I was up to it. I loved to test my strength and agility. Anything from five gallon buckets to feed sacks to chopping wood. The harder it was the better I liked it. I learned somewhere along the line to channel my anger and rage into my work. I do it to the best of my ability, but I liked to take things past the mark. I had to or it wasn't good enough for me. I wasn't good enough by my standards only. I learned to mutilate myself. I would hit a tree until my hands became like sausage. I would beat my head on things or slap or pinch myself. Sometimes I would scold myself like enough people weren't already doing it to me. I did get to a place where I realized I had to stop hurting myself. The pain let me know at least that I was still alive.

If it wasn't good enough, it was because I was too weak. So I had to get stronger. Somehow, that's when I picked up my first set of weights. It turned out to be the best high for me. It felt so good to put all that energy and rage into my physical self and then be able to release it. I became addicted to the weight lifting. I got too big in my arms and legs and too small in the waist for my regular clothes very quickly. I was fixing to have to make my own clothes when my daddy ordered me to stop lifting. I was beginning to look like a man. There was no doubt when you looked at me that I was a walking picture of strength.

Weight lifting brought on challenges that I had not expected from the men in my community. It got me raped twice. It got me beaten and burned. Men would challenge me to arm wrestling all the time. If I beat them they became enraged that a woman beat them.

I had the opportunity to go pro but I knew how my Daddy felt about it. It wasn't the life he had dreamed for me. I had no idea what he expected for me to pursue, but this wasn't it. I had been a permanent punching bag for my mom and siblings so what else could I aspire to? Seemed like a good match to me.

Godliness is
beneficial in
every way, since
it holds promise
for the present
life and also for
the life to come.
1 Timothy 4: 8

Chapter 12

I married at the tender age of 19 and soon gave birth to my son.

Mrs. Crawford made me worthy by teaching me how to be a wife and mother. I loved the married life until my husband started staying out late every night. I was left home alone like my mother tending to a baby. God only knows what he was doing. I guess I always picked the wrong man because I guess I considered that the normal way of life. It was all I ever knew.

We divorced after a few years. I missed the relationship with Mrs. Crawford more than anything. She was so good to me. I loved her dearly. She taught me everything I know about raising children. For that I'll always be thankful!

The lowliness that I expressed made it easy for people to take advantage of me. I am not a slave. I am not beneath them. They think I am nothing. Something that can be discarded in the trash. I've been a nobody long enough. I am a child of God! God has had His hand on me since birth. I would pray every night to God to just let me die. I wasn't meant for this world of evil. Then I realized I was here for a purpose and I had to seek that purpose out.

I let my guard down one night at a party and someone drugged my drink. Weeks later I found out that I was pregnant. This man was sent to prison because he had done this several times to other women. I never told my daughter his name because she didn't want to know someone who was sent to prison for raping women.

I was determined to be a productive human being even if it killed me. I wanted to be a great mom for my kids. Once my baby girl was born I didn't have time to pump iron. I was too busy trying to work and raise two small children. I was exhausted when I got home.

When Rayna was one year old I met Jim Davis and we got married. Jim was the only dad that Rayna ever knew and she loved him like no other. Jim and I didn't have a perfect marriage but then again who does? When you marry someone with baggage it makes for a very difficult journey for all involved. I felt like I was constantly being compared to his first wife. I felt inferior with no self-esteem. Having to deal with children from another marriage is also very difficult. Second marriages have a very low success rate. Something like a 60% failure rate. I was determined to have a successful marriage no matter what it took. Marriage counseling was in order.

Trust is a must in marriage and I couldn't trust anyone after the abuse I had endured. Is there any wonder why? Here is where the psychiatrist enters into the picture.

Talk about things getting very difficult to handle. This was the most painful time in my life having to relive those nightmares. You have to relive the memories in order to deal with them. You can't keep pushing them down. Reliving is a must.

"The Lord is my strength and my shield; my heart trusts in Him, and I am helped, therefore my heart rejoices, and I praise Him with my song."
Psalm 28: 7

Chapter 13

I have always heard that knowledge is power. I do believe it is true for this very reason. The key to defeating anything is to understand. You must fully understand the ins and outs of the subject matter or issues. So for that reason, I will attempt to explore each and every member of the group that lives within me.

I have always liked to get the hard stuff over with first because that leaves me with the gravy in the end. Now let's explore the most feared on my list, one of the two most inner dark personalities. They are never fully visible and yet at the same time never invisible.

Let's start with Mean. Mean forever more devises and invents schemes and booby traps. If there is a threat to the group, she has a plan. She is never without a solution to the situation. She always knows what to do and does it quickly, without a word or commotion. She moves quietly. She never asks the others for approval. Only the innocent one can stop her. She can set the stage, mastermind the play and then becomes the star actress. She is so good she can fool the best of them. Sometimes she regrets what she has done and goes away for awhile, but she will ever more scope the perimeter of the chamber. She never sleeps. She or he is the one to fear. There is nothing that can't be done by this one! She is a creation within herself. She likes that the others fear her. It feeds her power. She wants all the power and they fear her. She divides everything into levels. She has her own standards of levels. This is so that when the threat arises, she is ready to act. She knows the exact course that should be taken. Maybe they don't have time because Mean is so quick to the draw. She doesn't even waste a second. She knows the importance of timing. It's her greatest asset.

How did Mean come into existence? How do I know that Mean and the Protector are separate personalities? Let's say that on any ordinary day that I carry on normal functions in the real world. I go to work. I decide what to wear, meet, greet, and service every need that comes through my door. While I am talking to my customers, the group is talking and discussing the conversation as well. But they are not allowed to speak their opinions. They speak only to themselves. To the customer, I am only one person, but to me hidden inside is a whole group of other people talking at the same time as my customer. I hear all voices at once. It's a wonder how I've been able to deal with this all these years. Try to juggle everyday life with a group inside of you, esp. when you never know when a member of the group will appear.

It really is over whelming even to me when I look back and see so much more than what I feel I lived. For me to have survived such horrible events is a miracle. I should by all counts died by now. God just wouldn't let go of me and I glad He didn't. This is truly an extraordinary story to be able to tell. Only I can tell it!

I speak of these personalities and call them by name. They are real and everyday normalcy for me. They have all not been with me from the beginning. Some have joined me along the way. I will try to explain how they came into existence.

If you remember the horrible beating by my dad, that's when it happened for the first time. I suddenly found myself outside my body and nothing has been the same since. If I were in the medical business maybe I could explain things better but it was a way of my brain saving me.

There have been several times in my life with my husband that I know for sure Mean showed up and slept with Jim. She would take Beauty's place only in an emergency. She was forced a few times that I know of and a couple of times she just took over. Beauty and Mean are the only ones that sleep with Jim. I don't know how that would make him feel to know he has slept with the semi-same face for 15 years, and yet two totally different people.

On one occasion he has slept with three different people. What kind of life has he had to live in order to maintain a marriage? Oh my, darling husband. I hate to admit it but I think Jim enjoys sex with Mean instead of Beauty. I will leave the rest to your imagination.

Jim has seen Mean with his own eyes. He knows she exist. He tried to get me for years to look in the mirror, but I refused for years. One day, I got the courage to look in the mirror and I didn't recognize myself. There were marked differences. The color of my eyes were even different. My lips were smaller and my face shape was more square and my eyebrows were not even mine. It was like meeting a new person for the first time. This was my first glimpse of one of the group.

Jim demanded for Mean to leave. He told her he knew who she was and she was not welcomed here. He even said he hated her. He now knows the difference and can spot her in a heart beat. When he sees her coming, he leaves the area as quickly as possible. He even sneaks out sometimes before she can dig her claws into him. He has kept my secret for years. I don't think he knows how to explain it to someone anyway.

Mean induced those feelings and I am not sure why. Mean won't allow anyone to hurt her or the others. She keeps the innocent one hidden. She feels it's safer that way. So high are the walls in her fortress and that is by design. She doesn't want anyone getting it. Sometimes she allows the Innocent One to wander around outside the chamber but only for a brief moment. She is always present or very near. At all cost, the Innocent One must be protected and watch over. At the first sign of a threat, she will jerk the Innocent One back inside the chamber. It is a certain kind of threat that man himself requests Mean to come to the front. All holes within the chamber are sealed shut during the threat. If the group thinks the Innocent One will be hurt, they all go on high alert. All come together as one to protect her. The Innocent One belongs to God. He will give knowledge and understanding to help the soul survive. He helps the soul to be able to face the evil that wants in. Knowledge is power. He does not remove the physical pain or makes marks of evidence disappear.

The Innocent One feels the pain afterwards. All the evil that has been done will be deciphered and placed somewhere within the soul and sometimes with acceptance, it can be released all together. The truth will set you free. It feels like a butterfly that has been set free to float in the wind. Like a child playing at the feet of God. No worries, burdens, fears, or hunger. All is taken care of with the Lord. The deepest breath you will ever draw is the one after your soul has been cleansed by God. The bible is the written word of God and we can trust every word of it. Without God I am nobody.

The more I searched the pages of my wisdom, knowledge, and understanding, the more alive I became. I was numb and now I have feelings, love, and worth.

Jim opened his ears and heard her telling him her secrets. He sat on the edge of the bed and picked up her lifeless body and held her close to him and rocked her until she fell asleep. He laid her in the bed and then knelt down beside the bed and covered her with his body. The innocent one felt him praying. He was begging God to help her and to help him help her. Then she slept. Only God could have known the strength, patience, and love it would take to hold on to the Innocent One that night.

Jim won the unanimous vote of love from the group. They had never seen that kind of love. The group now has faith in his love and they can trust him. Now they are truly one.

Beauty is the one I feel most comfortable with. She is just what she says. She is beauty. She represents all things that are beautiful.

Beauty is seen in the environment and in people's faces and in their hearts. Beauty keeps the physical body clean. She gardens, keeps a clean house, loves to cook, sew, and do crafts. She is non-judgmental.

Beauty does all the physical labor in her job. She owns her own business while running another business as well. I guess you could say Beauty can do it all by herself. She keeps up with four kids, 5 grandchildren, three dogs, and a cat. She wears her heart on her sleeve. She loves everybody and all things, beautiful and right. She has a strong character and is good natured. She receives great pleasure from playing in the dirt. She is a pleasure to be around.

She's funny and witty. She makes her own party if there isn't one. She draws older people and babies close to her. She is a very good organizer. She can get things done in a hurry. She is the sole owner of her own business, which she built from the ground up. She does her very best at work and at home. She is full of compassion. She loves all children of all colors. She loves sunshine as well as rain. She loves to be near water but not in it. She loves makeup, ribbons, fishnet stockings, wolves, birdhouses, and colors.

Beauty has always gotten up early her whole married life to Jim.

Beauty loves to watch him sleep. She will lay next to him and listen to him breathe. She will kiss his hands and wait for his eyes to open. Beauty is the one that most people often meet. She stays at the front of the group and is in control of the group most of the time.

Weakness is the one I have dreaded. It's not good to dig too deep into Weakness. She cries all the time. She cries for all the others in the group and is crying right now because she doesn't want to do this. She stays in constant, everlasting prayer to God. She cries for the sins of herself and the group. She cries for the inflicted. She begs for forgiveness from God at all times. She's the hot link to God. She never stops worshipping Him. She never stops thanking God for all He has done for her, big or small.

The group likes to keep her near the back or outside the chamber. She is stuck in time space where she can not escape. She can not go forward or backwards. She only goes round and round. There is another reason she cries all the time. It's because she has been in the presence of the Lord. It's warm and almost child like. Innocent and free. A quiet place. A place you choose not to leave.

Weakness cries tears of shame, fear, joy, redemption, forgiveness, love, and loss. Weakness will forever more roam the perimeter of the chamber, toward the outside. Can you hear her cries? Her wailing? Her agonizing groans? Her cries are too annoying!

I have for some time now felt as though someone is sneaking up on me through a back door or by a secret passage. It's like being watched without knowing it. I fear Lea. The intruder may be coming in. Sweet little Lea. She has a very unique gift. The gift of the spirit. Where as she may be able to see spirits that surround her, most can not. Which one is the real me? Can I truly mesh them all into me? How will I know for sure? Who but God can help me? I will use God's written word and wisdom of all His angels. Mr. Altve, Mrs. Crawford, and Uncle Charlie are my angels. I will call upon all I have learned from all the people God placed in my life. I pray to God for wisdom, courage, and strength. I will try to use the real beauty of love as my foundation.

All of this in order to obtain true peace and tranquilly with in myself. I will make an attempt to make myself whole and worthy. I ask the Lord, my God Almighty to take this journey with me and to bring me back safe again. He is the only one who can. I trust that He will because I ask Him to. My God Almighty! Help me!!

The safest way I can figure to protect Lea for now is to stay clear of her until I can control the other ones within me or until Lea's mind becomes more mature. I love her and do not intend to harm her in anyway. I must keep hidden from her eyes as much as possible for her own protection. It is safe to say that this will probably freak out my husband because he does not know all the personalities inside of me. All these years he has thought there were only two and now there are six. See why I love him so much? God gave me the best husband for which I am forever grateful. His inner strength will matter much more for later on. I thank God for Jim.

Sometimes I feel like I have lived my life in reverse or maybe the trip backwards in time has made me feel that way. My brain tries to take over and run things, which is nothing more than a battle with the bitch inside of me.

My mind is brilliant and God knows this. The struggle with Weakness is continuous. She has not stopped since Mom got sick. In fact, she has been more persistent and louder than usual, which I take as a warning that something bad is about to happen. When that real bad gets here, I will need God's shield. I must remember this when my struggle becomes fierce.

No matter what, I will be as He decides it to be. God is all knowing and all powerful and He knows what's best for us. I must have control of my feelings and anger. I feel the rage building inside of me. I must not lose control. My struggle has already begun. Am I ready for the battle of my life? With God beside me, I'm ready for anything. All things are possible with Christ. Whether I go home or stay, that is God's decision not mine. I want to do God's will not mine.

The best laid plans
of kings have failed,
where God has not.
He is an all powerful,
awesome God in whom
we can depend and
trust.
unknown

Chapter 14

I worked until I couldn't go and do anymore. I nearly killed myself. I wasn't sleeping and eating right. I was going to die. I wasn't in my right mind or body. Exhaustion and malnutrition has raked my body. Once again God had to put me flat on my back. God had a plan and He needed my undivided attention.

The Dr. told us I would die before morning. Jim became a crutch for me to cling to and he didn't leave my side. I looked so awful that I felt sorry for Jim to have to look at me. He just sat in a chair by the hospital window and stared at me.

I knew for two weeks that I was going to die. I knew the moment the death angel visited me. I'll never forget how that felt. Spooky!

Two nurses came and took me for tests on my stomach. I was in some kind of x-ray room. I was surrounded by nurses and doctors. They handed me some chalky stuff to drink and told me to drink it in one long gulp. How in the world was I going to get this stuff down when

I haven't even been able to eat for weeks? I would like to see them do that. Well here goes nothing.

I told the nurses to move the wastebasket closer because I knew this was not going to stay down long. My stomach went into spasms and here it came with such force that it went across the room. Everyone was in shock.

There were two doctors, three nurses, and one tech standing there staring at me. All of a sudden, the doctor started screaming at the nurses to get me some medicine to help stop the vomiting.

The nurse was holding back my hair and supporting my head as I violently spewed blood straight across the room. I could not stop. It went on for eternity. Finally I started choking on something. I felt something in the back of my throat, and it was hung. I crammed two fingers down my throat and grabbed whatever it was and pulled. I couldn't talk and the nurse was trying to pull my hands away from my mouth. It had to get something out!

I tried to talk between gasps. I managed to get out the words, "I have worms!" The nurse put a cold rag on my forward and assured me that was no worm. It was the lining of my stomach! It looked like pink saran wrap. It looked like a thick balloon. My heart was doing flips from all the activity. I was exhausted! I collapsed back onto the table.

I woke up in the hall on a stretcher soaked with blood. I was in a line with a bunch of other people who were staring at me. I guess I looked like death. The spasms caused me to grunt. Why I don't know but at this point who cares. I started to get sick again but I couldn't talk to tell anyone to help me. The old man on the bed next to me screamed for help. I started vomiting blood again. Some one rolled me on my side as the blood poured down onto my bed and into my hair. I'm sure I looked like a bloody mess. Blood was everywhere!

I kept passing in and out of consciousness. Finally one little black girl came to my bed and I'll never forget her. She was so sweet. She rubbed my face with a cold wet rag. She looked me right in the face and said, "Honey, I don't know which room is yours but I'm going to take you right now to your room." Thank God for a sweet angel. Those poor people in the hallway looked scared to death. I'm sure I was a sight to see. Good thing I didn't have a mirror.

Jim had a horrible look on his face when I entered the room. Jim wanted to know what in the hell happened to me. I know I looked really bad because I had blood all over me. The poor girl didn't know. She just shrugged her shoulders and said she found me in the hallway.

That is when Jim did the most incredible thing. Without a word he reached down and scooped up my fragile, lifeless body into his arms and gently slid me off the bed. He held me till I fell asleep. He finally laid me back on my bed and covered me up. I heard him crying when he finally laid me back in my bed. I have never felt so loved in all my life. When I woke up Jim was still right there beside me. Over and over again Jim was the first thing I saw when I woke up. He was also the best thing I saw when my lights would fade into darkness.

That simple act of kindness and genuine love was all I needed.

Jim gave all he had to give. No one had ever cared about me to give all of themselves to me. It meant the world to me. It was what I needed to fight to live. He prayed so hard for God to let me live. His love has never been deeper since that day. I fed off his strength. I had no energy of my own so I pulled from his. The comfort and warmth of his body next to mine felt like heaven. His smell. His touch. I'm dying and all I can feel and hear is Jim. I wasn't aware of much that was going on but when Jim touched me I knew it was him. Nothing will ever come as close to me as Jim was that day. For once in my life I had someone who loved me as much as Christ loved me. I hope he knows how much I love him.

With Christ in the center of a marriage the way it is meant to be you become one with your partner. What a huge difference it makes in your joy and happiness. So many marriages fail because they don't put Christ first. Satan has destroyed so many families. That's why the divorce rates are so high.

Uncle Charlie came from Florida to be by my side. I could feel his hand on me and I could hear him talking to God on my behalf.

He taught me about humility and humbleness. He was the most influential person in my life besides my husband, of course. He was a godly man and had a very special relationship with God. There will never be another Charlie! God broke the mold when He made Uncle Charlie. I'll love him forever. He led me to Jesus Christ while sitting on my front porch. I will never be the same person again. A new creature in Christ am I. Healed from the inside out. Thank you God for sending your son Jesus Christ to die for my sins. Thank you God for grace! I am yours forever and ever.

The Lord also
will be a refuge
in times of
trouble.
Psalm 9: 9

Chapter 15

Two months after I got out of the hospital I was back at work. God pulled me through again, but then things began to happen. Everyday that went by I could see God opening all kinds of doors right before my very eyes. I told Jim about "the lady" who gave me a message. He felt funny inside and began watching and noticing the same things I was seeing. We both tried hard to figure out what it all meant.

Everything happens for a reason and nothing happens apart from God's knowledge. God has a purpose for everyone. It's up to you to figure out what that purpose is with God's help. You have to make sure who you are listening to. Satan is a master at deception. Remember he can take on many forms.

We have a lot of choices to make in life and it's up to you to make the right choices. So many times we run ahead of God and choose the path we like best which may not be the one God wants for you. Choose the wrong road and bad things will come your way. I pray for

God's will to be done because I've made too many wrong choices in life.

My smoking was a very bad choice. It may be too late, but I have to quit. There are always consequences to our actions. I take full responsibility for my smoking. I have found my purpose in life. I found it through "the lady" with her message from God for me.

This lady just walked through my salon doors one day and I have never seen her before. It was so surreal. It confirmed that I was here for a purpose.

I started working on my book. Nobody knew this but me, not even Jim. I've had a lot of experiences with people but this scared me. I've never had anyone just walk in and say they had a message from God before. At first I didn't believe her until she told me the message, then I knew it was from God. God had been preparing me for this last task for about two years. Things are getting pretty spooky.

This is a new road for me to travel. I know I am out of my element. I'm excited and scared at the same time. I know where God is leading me and I am not afraid. I totally trust Him. I know He is ever present with me, so what is there to fear? Where I am lacking in education He will provide. I am a willing servant.

I have no clue where to start or how to put together a book but He knows. That's all that matters. I'm just a willing servant ready to do what He would have me to do. Be a vessel and He will take it from there.

I speak a different language that no one else knows except for a select few like Uncle Charlie. It is my choice of words and the order I put them in. I call it artistic English. I can speak a word in a crowd and no one will know what I am really saying except for those who can also speak the special language. These people are attracted to me immediately and I will spot them by the look on their faces. We automatically know who we are. It's a true gift of gab.

Jim has come to understand it, even though he will never be able to speak it. Once I put my words on the internet, it will draw people to me who also speak this special language. I love what God is doing in my life. I knew someday I would write a book, when I was in the ninth grade and read my first literature. I didn't know how or what it would be about but I just felt it in my heart.

I've lived through many experiences and I was always a good listener. Most people just want someone to listen.

From the license to age of 29 years, I am constantly growing, learning, gaining integrity and respect. During this time I became very close to Jim's family. Uncle Charlie plays a huge role in our lives esp. our marriage. Uncle Charlie's prayers and righteousness restores my soul. I feel like I would not be here today without Uncle Charlie's petition to God to spare my life. We developed a very special relationship that only we know and understand. He prayed non stop for three days with his hand on me the whole time. When I woke up he was the first person I saw.

The weird part about this story is that Uncle Charlie was now speaking my special language. He had not been born with the gift but God gave it to him for his obedience and faithfulness. Jim was jealous that Uncle Charlie now had the gift of gab. He accepted it and in the end Uncle Charlie was able to offer Jim great comfort. Our relationship grew way beyond measure with Uncle Charlie's help.

Jim and I finally became one in spirit. Our love exists and thrives in God's magic. God sent Jim to me for my own personal happiness but God sent Uncle Charlie to me to teach me things in my own language. We spent 7 months together and each day he was teaching us new things. This is why I lost it when Uncle Charlie died. I felt like I had lost a huge part of my heart. It took me months just to get where I could function without him in my life. I spent a great deal of time going over and over what Uncle Charlie had taught me. He was a true friend who could connect with me and I had never had such a close friend before. It meant the world to me that he cared enough to love me. The last day I saw him he gave me my final instructions. What he wanted me to do when he was gone.

I was so broken down after that day knowing I would never see him again until it was my time to go home. As if that wasn't enough sadness, my dad died right before Charlie. I was spinning out of control with grief. It was so hard to lose two major loves in my life so close together. It rocked my world! I couldn't function.

I felt so alone. I had a huge void in my life.

Jim wished so bad that he could speak my language so he could comfort me. He did the only thing he knew to do and that was just to be by my side. Silent but there. I knew Jim felt my pain.

Because of His
strength will I
wait upon thee:
for God is my
defense.
Psalm 59: 9

Chapter 16

When Dad died, I'm proud to say he had been sober for several years and had found peace through Jesus Christ. Before he died, he gave special recognition of the truth for all to see. This meant so much to me in the healing process. He couldn't erase the damage done to me over the years but he did apologize to me with tears in his eyes. He had been misled and lied to by others. Who was he suppose to believe? Unfortunately, most people believe the words of an adult vs a child. There are ways to get to the bottom of things if one so desires. It takes an effort on the one seeking the truth.

I learned and understood love when my dad came down with cancer. Everything my dad had done for others came back full circle to him. It was amazing to see. He was repaid many times over when he could no longer work in the fields. God bless them for being the hands and feet of Christ.

Dad had about a thousand acres of corn in the ground that needed to be cut into silage. He could not afford to feed his cattle or pigs through the coming winter. After surgery and two years of chemo, Dad was not able to farm anymore.

One morning out of the blue, a week after dad's surgery, the ground began to shake like an earthquake. The windows were rattling and you could feel the floor moving beneath your feet. I have never witnessed such an incredible act of love in all my life. I ran to the window and couldn't believe my eyes. I helped Dad get to the window to see this miracle.

There was a long line of equipment headed our way. It was so awesome to watch. He couldn't believe what he saw. I think that day my dad learned there were two sides to humbleness. It was all the neighboring farmers and all their hired hands with their own equipment in an unbroken line with a solid mission to complete. What an awesome sight to behold! I've never seen anything like it again.

Together they cut, hauled, packed, and tied down all the silage in a week. It usually took Dad several weeks to complete on his own. And just as they came, they left in a single line right down the road back to their own farms. They disappeared into the sunset and the dust settled back down to the road. That was the biggest gift my dad had ever received. All who witnessed this extraordinary feat were blessed as well. How could one not be affected?

I took Daddy for granted in so many ways but I always respected and revered him as an earthly father that had faults just like anyone else. I loved him more than words can ever express. I received cards and calls of condolences from people from all over the county. The flower shops could not fill all the orders that came in and the outage of flowers covered three counties.

Even my Mom received a letter from the House of Representatives informing her that they had taken the day off in honor of my dad. I still have that letter till this day. My dad had earned a lot of respect over his lifetime. I'll always be so proud to call him Dad. I hate to think what my life would have been like if he had chosen not to love me like the others in my family. I couldn't have bared it!

My dad spent his life trying to protect me from my mom. He did the best he knew how to do with the information that he had.

For I know the
thoughts that I
think toward you,
saith the Lord,
thoughts of peace,
and not of evil,
to give you an
expected end.
Jeremiah 29: 11

Chapter 17

It's a hard pill to swallow when you know that your mother hates you with every ounce of her being. I went to the hospital to see her when I was told she was dying. I walked in the room and when our eyes met, she told me to get the hell out of her face. I turned and walked out into the hall. Shortly there after, she drew her last breath. My life long dream was that she would somehow manage to love me, but that wasn't possible for her. I didn't have any control over who I looked like. She couldn't bring herself to judge me for my character and substance instead of my beauty. I'm glad I got my looks from my dad. It was Mom's problem not mine.

It's bad being hated from birth but to still be hated at Mom's death bothered me for years. When someone hates you at death there is no room or time to resolve the issues. I realize now that Mother never was going to change no matter how many years had passed. You must accept facts and move forward or your heart will be shredded into a pulp and you will suffer a miserable life. I no longer would allow her to control my emotions because she was messed up. God helped me deal with the cold hard facts. You have to openly and honestly give your burdens to God. Put them at the foot of the cross and walk away from them. Just don't make the mistake of picking them back up again. This takes strong will power and control. God is waiting to take your burdens from you. He doesn't want you to be sad. You are His child. He wants you to be happy. He wants you to be free to do His work and not burdened under a heavy load of problems. Remember it's not about you. This world is all about Jesus. Thank God everyday that we are closer and closer to seeing Him in the sky to take us home. Amen! Mom is paying dearly for her sins right now. She had a long time to change her mind but in the end she chose not to accept Jesus Christ as her Lord and Savior. That is the unforgiveable sin. Jesus' love for you kept Him on the cross. What have you done for Him? He gave up his life for you. What an awesome sacrifice Christ gave for you. He took on all the sins of the world when He didn't have to. How does that make you feel knowing your sins were added to Jesus's back as He hung there on the cross?

For God so loved the
world, that He gave His
only begotten Son,
that whosoever
believeth in Him
should not perish,
but have everlasting
life.
John 3: 16

Chapter 18

Being forced and threatened to keep my mouth shut put a timer on my ticking bomb. My subconscious was aware of the timer, but for some reason it refused to admit or allow the memories to fully surface.

After Mom died the memories started flooding back. The very one who was suppose to love me, hated my guts. She placed the muzzle on my mouth. God forbid that the family loses respect. Give me a break! The anger that got bottled up inside of me became fitful rage. Then it turned into disgust, loathe, and pure raw hatred. None of them hated me as much as I hated myself. I wondered why they didn't just drag me out to the woods and lynch me. They could have saved me a ton of heartache and pain. The lynching would have been quicker and probably a lot less painful.

They chose to kill me slowly from the inside out. A slow painful death. I can't tell you how many times I begged God to take me home. Remove me from this living HELL! I was smothering. Half of me wanted to live while the other half wanted to die. I had no control.

I couldn't run away. We had family all around me. I couldn't hide. Nobody wanted me. Why didn't someone call the law? Why didn't my teachers notice the bruises? I fell through the cracks and no one cared.

Years later when I read *The Scarlet Letter*, she wore her shame on the outside for all to see, while mine was hidden inside. I suffered three times if not more than she did. My life was quite the opposite. No happy ending for me. I wondered if someone painted me a big red sign and hung it around my neck if anyone would notice or care.

Why did all the dirty people pick me out? Was it because I was singled out from the family? Was it because I was always playing alone and it would be easy to grab me or was it because no one cared what happened to me? Maybe it's a combination of all of the above.

I felt like I was the hunted. That's exactly what the muzzle did to me. It made me an easy pick because they knew I wouldn't tell and then who would have believed me? Nobody ever listened to me anyway.

It was the rage that created Mean. By the time, I figured out who she was, she was well established. You have probably figured out by now that Mean was the "Queen" of the bus. Duh!

Thank goodness we don't get all the bad memories at once. If I had, I probably would have died of a cardiac arrest. Even at a little at a time I still had a very difficult time dealing with all the damage. To this day, I still feel the repercussions of those times. Regardless of what others did to me, God was with me every step of the way. He placed so many saints along the way to teach me about love and acceptance that I couldn't get at home from my own flesh and blood. God has never forsaken me. He never gave up on me, even though there were times I turned my back on Him. God has done great and magnificent things for me. I had rather look at the good instead of the negative. What kind of life is one filled with regrets and pity? That is not a life to me. I want to live life to its fullest. Seize the day while you can.

It doesn't matter
where you go in life.
It's whom you have
beside you.
unknown

Chapter 19

One day I was working on the computer, deciding on a name for my website and what all would be on the site. I started coughing and couldn't stop. All of a sudden something flew out of my mouth. When I took a closer look I realized it was a chunk on my lung. Every cough after that was blood. I called a friend and she came right over. She rushed me to Memphis, TN where I had a friend that worked at the hospital.

Jim was working three counties away but as soon as we called him, he headed to Memphis. He made it in record time. It was in Memphis that I learned I had non small cell lung cancer. What a blow to hear that dreaded word cancer! I guess that I could have thrown up my hands and given up. Does that sound like me? Nope! God has already overcome the world. He can handle what we can't. I knew where I was going once I finished here. I just didn't feel like I had finished what He had for me. God's timing is perfect so why fret over a word. I've cheated death many times so why should this task be any different.

God holds me in His hands every day, every minute of the day. I'm in good company. With the news came a 4-5 % chance of survival. My what low odds! Somebody cut me a break. How did this happen? I'm sure my smoking for 35 plus years didn't help. I knew the risk when I started. I'm also sure growing up under cotton sprayings didn't help either. Then there are cleaning fluids and hair salon chemicals. What have I done? What I am about to go through is nothing compared to what I have already been through. God has snatched me from the hands of the Death Angel three times already for His purposes.

No, I'm not made of steel, but God is my shield and protector. God's will be done! Now comes another breakdown for my body. I know I will suffer greatly because I am strong in the Lord. Satan loves to come after us because he can't have our souls. Hit the road Satan. Your day of reckoning is coming soon!

So you want to know what I've been doing since I got home from the hospital? I have been gathering my materials, tightening my words, and getting my references indexed. I'm carrying right on with living. I will not stop or slow down until God tells me to. I will suffer and I will look bad for awhile. I will lose my hair and that's sad, but it will grow back. I'll lose my butt, but hey, that's a good thing.

I am hereby officially a retired beautician and at the same time a budding artist of words. Go figure! God closes doors and at the same time he opens windows. God has my undivided attention. I am a medical impossibility. The doctors agree that my condition is very rare. I'm built, strong like a man because I worked beside by Dad and lifted iron. I have amazing external muscles and my interior muscles are like those of three physically fit men. No matter how you slice me, I have no other symptoms.

My left lung is as healthy as someone twice as young as me and one who has never smoked a day in their life. Get that! Wow, I'm a superwoman that is dying! Ever heard of that? My outlook and my physical strength combined with no other symptoms are medically impossible. Now that word impossible, fits my life perfectly. I really do, do the impossible. Satan loves the word impossible. I know all things are possible with God and Satan can't compete with God. Remember Satan tried to take God's place in heaven and look what happened to him.

The real danger lies in the fact that cancer has spread to the main artery from the lung to my heart. Any jolt to my heart could cause the artery to rupture. I have a collapsed lung because of the tumor in my airway. I have a yeast infection in my mouth from the antibiotics, bed sores on my tailbone, hemorrhoids from the strain of the pain, swollen hands and feet from the fluid, and I now weigh under a hundred pounds. Like that isn't enough.

I don't consider this a trial. It's an opportunity for God to show His greatness. It's more of an honor than a curse. Bet you never heard anyone say that before. I live for God. He is my heavenly father of which I am very proud to belong to a king. I am not afraid to die. Only afraid of what they might do to me to make me live. There are worse things than death.

There are churches in five states that are lifting me up to our Lord. Thousands of people are praying for this little country girl from a one horse town. I ain't going down without a fight! I ain't going down till the fat lady sings. I'll probably trip her on her way up to the stage! If that doesn't work, don't be surprised if I mule kick her!

It is God's will that everyone be saved. I am saved and for that reason alone, I am not afraid to die. To live is to suffer in this evil, broken world. As my time draws nearer, I long for the comforts of heaven. That causes my heart to jump for joy. At the same time my family is devastated. I do not wish to leave Jim. He is my one true love of my life. My best friend forever. I'll save him a seat under the biggest shade tree in heaven. God has already shown me what Jim's love is capable of. With his love and arms around me, I will be safe and happy even if God chooses to take me home. We have learned over time that we are only passing through this world. I will be glad to hear Jesus say, "Welcome home my faithful servant."

It's a test of unbelievable proportion. A leap of faith such as I have never taken before. Jim and I decided to seek medical treatment in Mexico. They have drugs that we don't have, so here we go. Along with healthy eating and vitamin B17 I manage to reject the cancer in my right lung. After weeks of treatment we head home. We returned to rural Mississippi and weeks later I feel a very small bump in my neck. I'm talking the size of a BB. After Dr. Spears did the biopsy on the bump, it doubled in size in a week. Jim and I returned to Mexico to receive treatments on the lymph nodes. I receive injections in my neck and I feel really bad. Jim keeps talking about returning home to work. We need the income. I don't want him to leave me down there. I need him with me. You have to stay on the US side and take the bus over the border for treatments. How am I going to do this alone? God it's just you and me on this journey. I need to feel your presence.

I'm waiting for Jim to return from the clinic. The border has been closed due to the swine flu. We are trying to decide if we need to return to home in Mississippi. If I can't cross the border, who is going to remove my port? I can't keep it in for a month. It has to be changed weekly. God help us to know what you would have us to do. Help!

All the cancer books I've been reading encourages eating organic foods. I need to purify my body after 45 years of abuse and eating the processed foods. I must learn to meditate to help control my pain. Positive thinking is a must. No time for pity parties. I'm having trouble eating. I'm not hunger but I know I need my strength. No food, no bowel movements. I need Jim to come get me and take me back to Mississippi. I have used all the information that I can find. If it's my time to go then nothing can keep me here. I trust God because He knows what's best. I hate to leave loved ones behind but I can't take them with me. They will follow when it's their time. I'll be waiting to see you at the gate!

I spend my time thinking of happier days on the farm catching tadpoles, frogs, lightening bugs, and rolling down the hills and valleys on our property. Rolling in old tires and swinging from vines. My peace I created in the woods was my favorite times as a child. Wonder what there will be to do in heaven? Whatever it is there will be total and complete peace. God says, "Peace I give to you."

Bonnie Davis passed from this life to an eternal life in paradise with her heavenly father Jesus Christ on July 9, 2009. Bonnie had her children and husband by her side when she left this world.

Bonnie was an extraordinary person. Her doctor said it was the most severe case of abuse he had ever seen. Most people don't live long from a severe case of abuse. I know in my heart I couldn't have withstood that kind of abuse. I would have died of a broken heart if my mother didn't love me. My mother was everything to me. I can't wait to meet Bonnie in heaven where everything is perfect. No sorrow, pain, or suffering!! Whatever your burdens are, lay them at the foot of the cross and let Jesus have them. He is waiting on you. Put them down and don't dare pick them up again. Would love to hear from you. You can email me at vera.gaines@att.net. This is the first day of the rest of your life. Live it well.

Life isn't about
waiting for the storm
to pass. It's about
learning to dance
in the rain.
unknown

AFTERWARDS

Bonnie left this world with her children and her husband Jim by her side. She lived in rural Mississippi her whole life. She was a trained beautician and loved life and the many people she crossed paths with. She never knew a stranger. Bonnie would do anything she could for you if she thought she could make your life richer. She was married to Jim Davis for 17 years. The love of her life. How many of us have the privilege to say we married our soul mate?

Bonnie's main goal in life was to help those who have been abused to live a free and happy life despite their past. Most of all she wanted to lead people to Christ. Bonnie survived her abuse by the grace of God. He is always with you and will never forsake you. Bonnie is in heaven praying for you and your loved ones right now. Remember her sitting at the feet of Jesus Christ. Look her up when you arrive and tell her you read her book. It is a dream completed!

Bonnie is a heroine in my book, right up there with Joan of Arc.

Such courage and determination from such a small woman with a huge heart. She probably falls in the top 99 percentile. So rare but just so down to earth. She watched after the underdog, the less fortunate, and the children. That tells her character right there.

She basically educated herself. If she didn't know something she would research it. There wasn't much she couldn't do. If I had lived near her, I know we would have been close friends. We loved the outdoors, animals and babies. We grew up in adjoining counties in Mississippi. I related to a lot she described in the days of old even though I am older by about 9 years. Thank you Jim for trusting me with Bonnie's most private notes and thoughts. Also thanks for your patience. It was well worth the wait. I'm sure we will see the fruits of Bonnie's labor. Everything we do to further the kingdom plants seeds even if we don't live to see the results.

Every time I think I'm having a bad day, I remember Bonnie and I immediately confess that I'm having a good day compared to Bonnie's life. Go forth and rejoice for this is the day that the Lord hath made!

CANCER

What cancer can not do . . . .
It can not invade the soul,
suppress memories,
kill friendships,
destroy peace,
conquer the spirit,
shatter hope,
cripple love,
corrode faith,
steal eternal life,
silence courage.
unknown

The Greatest Stories of the Bible

The Creation Story—Genesis 1:1, 2:7

The Fall of Man—Genesis 3:6-24

The Flood—Genesis 6:1-9, 9:17

The Call of Abraham—Genesis 12:1-9

The Ten Commandments—Exodus 20:1-17

The Shepherd's Plan—Psalm 23

The Birth Of Christ—Matthew 1:18, 2:23,Luke 1:26, 2:40

The Sermon on the Mount—Matthew 5-7

The Beatitudes—Matthew 5: 3-11

The Lord's Prayer—Matthew 6: 9-15, Luke 11:2-4

The Prodigal Son—Luke 15:11-23

The Good Samaritan—Luke 10: 29-37

Psalm Sunday—Like 19: 28-44

The Last Supper—Matthew 26: 20-25, Mark 14:12-26

The Garden of Gethsemane—Matthew 26: 36-46

The Betrayal of Jesus—Matthew 26: 47-56

The Death of Christ—Luke 23: 26-56, John 19: 16-42

The Resurrection of Christ—John20,Luke 24,Matthew 28

The Ascension—Acts 1: 1-12

The Advent of the Holy Spirit—Acts 2: 1-21

Live each day to the fullest. Get the most from each hour, each day, and each age of your life. Then you can look forward with confidence, and back without regrets. Be yourself—but be your best self. Dare to be different and follow your own star. And don't be afraid to be happy. Enjoy what is beautiful. Love with all your heart and soul. Believe that those you love—love you. Forget what you have done for your friends, and remember what they have done for you. Disregard what the world owes you and concentrate on what you owe the world. When you are faced with a decision, make that decision as wisely as possible—then forget it. The moment of absolute certainty never arrives. And above all, remember that God helps those who help themselves. Act as if everything depended upon you, and pray as if everything depended upon God.

S. H. Payer

HEALING PROMISES

By Jesus' stripes I am healed. (1 Peter 2: 24)

It is God's will that I prosper and be in good health, just as my soul prospers. (3 John 2)

The Lord is my healer: (Exodus 15: 26)

Jesus came that I may enjoy life and have it in overflowing abundance. (John 10: 10)

As I serve the Lord, sickness is taken from my midst. (Exodus 23:25)

Healing is one of God's benefits. (Psalm 103: 3)

Jesus is the serpent of the pole lifted up in the New Covenant for my healing and deliverance. (John 3:14)

God sent His word and healed me. (Psalm 107: 20)

I pay attention to God's word, for it is life to my body and health to my flesh. (Proverbs 4: 20-22)

God gives me good and perfect gifts. He has no sickness or disease to give me. (James 1: 17)

As I submit to God and resist the devil, he must flee from me. Sickness and disease must flee from me. (James 4: 7)

Jesus is able and willing to heal me. (Matthew 8: 1-20)

Jesus can heal me through my believing, receiving, and speaking His word or through the touch of another believer who is empowered by the Holy Spirit. (Mark 16: 18)

Jesus paid for all sin and sickness at Calvary. (Matthew 8: 17)

Jesus is the same yesterday, today, and forever. (Hebrews 13: 8)

Because the Lord is my refuge and habitation, no evil nor plaque shall come nigh my dwelling. (Psalm 91: 9-11)

I am redeemed with the blood of Jesus Christ. (1 Peter 1: 19)

I am justified by faith, not by words of the law. (Galatians 3: 13)

Jesus redeemed me from the curse of the law. (Galatians 3: 13)

The blessings of Abraham have come upon me. (Deuteronomy 28: 1-14)

Jesus legally redeemed me from the bondage of sickness and disease and every other work of the enemy. (Luke 13: 10-17)

Jesus bore my grieves (sickness) and carried my sorrows (pain). (Isaiah 53:4)

Jesus was wounded, bruised, and beaten for my sins, sickness, and diseases. (Isaiah 53: 5)

I discern the Lord's body and receive all that He has provided for me, including healing for my physical body. (1 Corinthians 11: 23-30)

The resurrection power of Jesus Christ flows from my tongue as I speak words of life. (Proverbs 18: 21)

I have been given authority in the name of Jesus to speak to the mountains that I face. As I command the mountains of sickness, despair, hopelessness, and lack to be removed in Jesus' name, they must go and be replaced with the fullest of God's blessings. (Mark 11: 22,23)

Because I meditate on the word of God day and night, God's prosperity and success are overtaking me in all realms of life. (Joshua 1: 8)

Jesus is moved with compassion on my behalf. He wants me healed because of His great love for me. (Matthew 14: 14)

Satan cannot dominate or oppress my life, because Jesus came to set me free. (1 John 3: 8) (Acts 10: 38)

Just as God's grace was sufficient to cause Paul to overcome all of Satan's buffetings. Christ Jesus causes me to triumph in every area of life. (2 Corinthians 12; 9, 10)

I will rise above anything and everything the devil throws at me. Nothing can keep me down, for I am more than a conqueror in Christ Jesus. (Romans 8: 35-39)

Today I will rise to new life from the depression and prostration in which circumstances have kept me. (Isaiah 60: 1)

Jesus is the author of abundant life, while it is Satan who steals, kills, and destroys. (John 10: 10)

The days of my life are seventy years and if by reason of strength eighty. (Psalms 90: 10)

Long life is mine because I obey and honor my parents in the Lord. (Ephesians 6: 1-3)(Exodus 20: 12)

My obedience to the Lord prolongs my life. (Proverbs 10: 27)

ABOUT THE COAUTHOR

Vera Simpson Gaines was reared on a dairy farm outside of Houston, MS. She attended Houston High School and then went to Miss. State Un. where she graduated in Elem. Ed. She taught school for 7 years and then moved into educational research. Gaines resides in Senatobia, MS with her husband Gary of 43 yrs. She has two daughters Dr. Heather Gaines Hardison of Collierville, TN and Tiffany Gaines Lambert from Olive Branch, MS.

Gaines wrote her first book, *Call Me Jobulene* as an autobiography about her trials and tribulations and how she overcame them with the help of God. Her second book *Are You A Job In Modern Times?* is for the Katrina victims since she lost her grandmother indirectly from Camile. Her third book *All Is Well With My Soul* is a daily devotional. Gaines is currently working on *There's A Spy Among Us* with her brother Don Simpson.

Books can be ordered online at www.authorhouse.com. Because Bonnie is not here to promote her book, why not help her to reach the abused and unsaved by ordering others a copy of this book. Further the kingdom by passing on Bonnie's book. You will be blessed for it.

Remember that a bible that is falling apart is usually owned by someone who's not. My prayer is that you were blessed by reading this story of Bonnie Davis' life. God bless you!

ALL IS WELL WITH MY SOUL

DAILY DEVOTIONS

VERA SIMPSON GAINES

Are You A Job
In Modern Times?

Study Guide Included

VERA SIMPSON GAINES

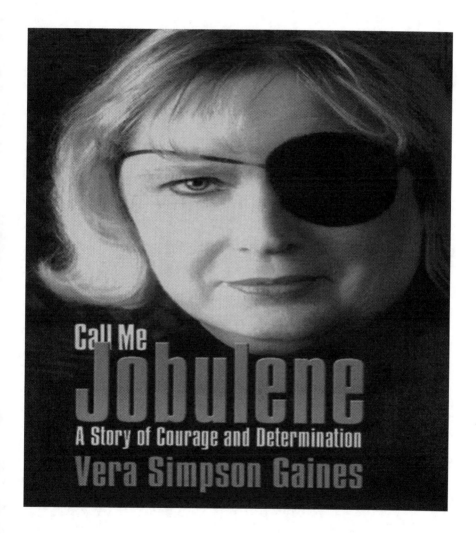

Call Me
Jobulene
A Story of Courage and Determination
Vera Simpson Gaines

NEVER BORROW SORROW
FROM TOMORROW

Deal only with the present,
Never step into tomorrow,
For God asks us just to trust Him
And to never borrow sorrow-
For the future is not ours to know
And it may never be,
So let us live and give our best
And give it lavishly-
For to meet tomorrow's troubles
Before they are even ours
Is to anticipate the Saviour
And to doubt His all-wise powers-
So let us be content to solve
Our problems one by one,
Asking nothing of tomorrow
Except "THY WILL BE DONE."

Helen Steiner Rice

THE SOUL, LIKE NATURE, HAS SEASONS, TOO

When you feel cast down and despondently sad
And you long to be happy and carefree and glad,
Do you ask yourself, as I so often do,
Why must there be days that are cheerless and blue?
Why is the song silenced
In the heart that was gay?
And ask God, "What makes life this way?"
And His explanation makes everything clear,
The Soul has its seasons the same as the year,
Man, too, must pass through life's autumn of death
And have his heart frozen by winter's cold breath-
But Spring always comes with new life and birth
Followed by Summer to warm the soft earth-
And, oh, what a comfort to know these are reasons
That souls, like Nature,
Must too have their seasons,
Bounteous Seasons and Barren Ones, too

Times for Rejoicing and Times to be blue-
For with nothing but "Sameness" how dull life would be
For only life's challenge can set the soul free,
And it takes a mixture of both Bitter and Sweet
To Season Our Lives and make them complete.

Helen Steiner Rice

YESTERDAY . . . TODAY . . . AND TOMORROW!

Yesterday's dead, Tomorrow's unknown,
So there's nothing to fear and nothing to mourn,
For all that is past and all that has been
Can never return to be lived once again-
And what lies ahead or the things that will be
Are still in God's hands so it is not up to me
To live in the future-that is God's great unknown
For the past and the present God claims for His own,
So all I need do is live for Today
And trust God to show me The Truth and The Way-
For it's only the memory,
Of things that have been
And expecting tomorrow
To bring trouble again
That fills my Today,
Which God wants to bless,
With certain fears

And borrowed distress-
For all I need live for
Is this one little minute
For life's HERE and NOW
And Eternity's in it.

Helen Steiner Rice